Published by Polari Press
polari.com @polaripress

ISBN: 978-1-914237-03-4

Printed by Severn, Gloucester
Typeset in 10/12 Roslindale.

Cover design and typesetting
by Peter Collins for Polari

Edited by Tahnee Cadrez Freda

This first edition was printed in
the UK in November 2021

HOT
TEARS
THROUGH
VELVET
RAGE

ADRIANN
RAMIREZ

polari

CONTENTS

Dedicated to all of the angels who walk amongst us.

And to whoever comes across this book and takes the time to read it. I hope these words transcend my own experience and find you exactly where you are, where you have been and where you are going.

FOREWORD
PAUL KINDERSLEY

It was one of those magical moments of synchronicity that I got to know Adriann, and now on picking up this book you too will have the pleasure. Kind and exciting, open and enthusiastic, like Adriann's captivating course through life, a beat pulses and dances through these pages. Cute rhymes, quinces and medlars jostle with complex sentences, tarot cards and roses, all punctuated with snapshots of a life full of light, colour and an obsession with detail. Lime, pink, orange & caramel infiltrate and titillate, not one of our senses left untouched.

The seemingly frivolous temporality of berries and flowers takes on a passionate significance as Adriann takes us firmly by the hand and leads us deeper into ourselves to question our surroundings, our food, our every minute actions and their consequences. We enter a world where perhaps it is religion, shame and their public obloquy that should be made trivial and the mysterious majesty of a pomegranate or sunset all powerful – as Adriann swings us between the two like a beautiful acrobat we reassess accepted hierarchies and examine where and how we spend our energy and time. We discover a place anchored in transience and movement rather than hardened destination.

Not afraid to be personal, embracing encounters from Mexico to California to Hampstead Heath, the poems rattle with meals enjoyed, tears shed and names recalled and forgotten. We are introduced to Oscar, Lilith, Irving, Jose, Father Ed, Mike, Casey, Toni, Monika, Merci, Nina, Marilyn, to men in cars and lovers real and imagined. Each name a spark ignited as we catch a glimpse of a life entwined and like the rosehips and blood red peaches pressed between Adriann's manicured fingertips they stay with us as his voice feeds us clues and experiences. Characters populating a vivid crystalline dreamscape anchored in visceral experience.

All drenched in a pink light the poems sparkle as they bring people together through their rhythm and flow, a voice inquisitive but never intimidated. A sexy, sweaty yet secure nightclub of images and phrases – always full of wonder and trust, a quality so rare in times when we are taught to fear. The poems remind us of our complexity as we smile and cry, laugh and experience pain, abuse each other and love one-another - all in one day, all in one stanza, all in the blink of an eye or the bite of an apple. Adriann's prose captures that human ability to be all things at once.

July 2021

I.

Hot tears through velvet rage
For the boy I used to be
And for the person I became

HOLLY SUGAR

I left green quince in the bowl until they turned yellow
Till their scent went from mellow
to sweet, pungent marshmallow
like Sharon's favorite subtle pomelo
While the autumn sun began to amble
across our living room and long candles
I sat in the sun as much as I could handle

Few cherries bleed like the ones in tall glass jars

I like how in the autumn, the afternoons feel like morning
until it's suddenly dark
Birds sing earlier
Little apples grow on trees
on the side of the road
once pollinated by bees in the spring

You see Jose,
The desert would never suit me in the way
The way it does you
The arid nature of the air you grew up in created the
perfect climate to see you grow
But for me, left me stifled and stunted my growth
Only seeing myself in the graffitied mural of the Virgin
Mother on the wall near the Hostess Cake shop
near the train tracks on the East Side
Freight railcars blowing through all stops
that I used to listen to in the middle of the night
Dreaming of how they'd take me away one day
And how this perpetual state of feeling misunderstood
would finally be at bay

Looking up at the top of the Holly Sugar silos every winter
Seeing the two stars lit up, red and green
Glittering and untouchable
Kinda like how I saw myself to be

Now I can walk to the Heath and get lost in the sea of green
Disappear and finally let go, walk for ages without being seen

In our valley, the land was so flat you could see for miles
From our little home all the way to Mexico
Completely exposed
And you with your top shelf tequila always on the go

You cried on the phone when I said I love you
I guess there was something in my sentiment that didn't
ring true
But when I think of the wild and sweet fennel blowing in
the breeze
growing alongside California's highways
I think of you and how you could only love me in your way
And when I go home, it doesn't feel like home anymore
because I'm now comfortable there
The roads are wider and I can breathe in the same arid air
As you
I can look at the mountains in Mexico from where I stand in
California and not feel the divide
I put my arms through the bars at Friendship Park and
finally embrace myself

TRAVELED FRUIT

I am traveled fruit
Like the fruit in stands on the street I walk by
In rows and rows
Exotic and piled high
But I am not exotic, do not call me exotic like the fruit that
towers
I am not a fruit that can be purchased or eaten
But a fruit to be won and devoured

And sometimes I spend money
Just to spend money
Just to feel something
So I pick a peach, a blood peach
that tastes like strawberries and lime
speaking Spanish and lying
And that's me
Because who am I but a fruit that started out as a bud
which blossomed
into a flower which then died
Only to become a fruit
Unripened at the height of summer
To go ripe and ready in the autumn light
To ultimately be devoured in the limelight

TELL THEM ABOUT THE SKY

Walk towards the light I say
Which also happens to be the muddiest path
But tell them about the sky
Tell them how if you want the answers to all of your
problems all you have to do is look up high
And while the sun hits your face
The light gives you its answer and with no tan or trace
You're wiser than you were a mere five seconds before
Instead of scrounging for meaning on the kitchen floor
Pick yourself up, stand tall and count to four
And

Tell them about the sky
It's so obvious it's been there every season
The answers are their bodies which they've hated for no
reason
Tell them that even if you catch your glance in the mirror
for a moment and like what you see
Your reflection is a real thing and it can be everything you
ever dreamed
That is, only if what you see is what's in front of you and
not what you wish it'd be
And

Tell them about the sky
I urge you to stop searching for all of the reasons why
You are here now
Feel your skin in this light and be thankful to be alive
Every hard moment in your life you've survived
Say "Thank you! I'm grateful!" and drown your sins in lye

But anyway,
I wish the man standing in front of Seven Sisters Road
station would stop yelling all of this into his microphone
God rejected me and my desires long ago
and while Jesus may have died for somebody's sins
He must've forgotten about mine
And I'm sure Eve was just up for a bit of fun
because the quince she took the bite out of looked more
enticing than an eternity spent with Adam

Maybe if you got a better sound system next time I'd stay
and listen
Instead I look down to the black pond which reflects my
singular transmission
Every notch I've carved into my heart like ripples on the
surface
I stop, take a moment and make my first assertive
decision
I look to the sky, and yes I do see the golden light
but I search for no answers nor do I ask why
Angels who walk amongst us direct me towards the right
path
not self righteous or judgmental when my faith wavers or
ceases to last

And when I go wayward of the heart towards spring's
natural end
Here come the swifts every summer listening to their
internal clock that's ticking every second
No need for mortal men with microphones on the corner
for direction
Never touching ground for fear they'll never take off again
Only blind faith in themselves and blind faith in the wind
They know the sky
It is their home
and those answers only come from within

LAVENDER COUNTRY

Country is mine
but the country is not mine
And in Lavender Country, I know it's of the divine

Cocksuckin' Blues
those honky tonk tunes
finally some sad songs for me to dance along to

MY ADONIS

Adonis, my Adonis
On the dance floor I am sweating
Loving the anonymity
The red light on my body
The picture of a desperate man with his shorts at his
ankles
Shuffling around looking for another boy to love him if
they're able
With their greedy mouths for the greedy lout
His leather strap in my hands
The leather strap on his back

You are motherless, let me be your mother
You are fatherless, I can be your daddy
I want to cradle him like my child
Selfish and unknowing like an infant
Care for him, maybe like a brother
Heal him, kiss him
Maybe change his life in an instant

Si muero, entonces muero
No me digas nada, porque yo te quiero

And like the roses gave way to the hydrangea in the late
summer sun
his masked swish gives way to me
How he longs to be me
To be free like me
To inhabit both strength and fragility like me
To be free

Adonis, my Adonis
I see you fading in that same red light
the one in which you used to shine so bright
Is it sweat or is it tears?
Love with no fear, cause I'll still be here
And when the decade ends your friendships,
all you knew and fell in love with
You'll remember this night with an ache
Adonis, you'll look back and ponder the Great White Way,
my love and your fate

WHITE HOT FOREVER

Rebel
Heather
Heaven Hill
Head laying sideways on the windowsill

Cautious
Blowing
Soft in the wind
Visions of mother, tomatoes in tin

White
Hot
White hot forever
How many times will you remind me until I finally
remember?

Brown, pink auras
Visions through absence of light
Slept on the couch next to me night after night

Mumbling
Dropping
Your hand in my mouth
Numbers and colors swirling, I've lost count

Endless
Summer
The smell of that church basement
Randy, you held me through my own bereavement

Turquoise
Silver
Stones going missing in the night
Little wishes I sent to you quietly, taken with your light

Violet
Almond
Bed linen in sun
Instead of answering you, I packed my stuff to run

ON SLAYING

Don't you get it yet?
I do not slay for your entertainment
I do not own these streets so you can snap your fingers
at me in support
I am not fierce for you
I am not your mother, do not call me your mother
white girl

To slay by definition is a violent description
A massacre, in defense
One slays their enemies
And aren't you?
In war, the long war
the one I've been fighting since I was born

How violent I wish to be
to even feel an ounce of the hate that's been shown to me

DEADHEAD

Yellow gingham on the table
On the TV, Spanish fables
Medlars ripening in the late summer sun
Softening and sweetening in their ageing
But convince me that we still have fun
Convince me that our domestic lives are what we always
wanted
And that going to bed at a reasonable hour beats being
bent over a stranger's car bonnet

Because the beautiful men on their fast bikes scare me
And the trill of their guitars excite me
The sirens I hear are reverberating through the trees
But I don't know where they're coming from
And I miss my walking and my freedom
My thoughts meandering, no need to lead them

So many peach stones on the floor
They follow me
Leading the path to a tall oak tree
Surrounded by dozens of votive candles that once
glittered softly
For a life lived then lost only to live again beyond the
seams
of reality
One last blossom in the sea of berries
The last one left on these once fruitful trees

Summer's coming to an end
I should've known
I always get sad when the sun goes down quicker
and it gets colder
My walks get shorter
And the animals bolder
But I don't feel any smarter

I just feel older

And so I begin to think
What do I learn when the mistakes feel comforting?
Mistake my sadness for a friend that feels nurturing?
Who could I be without that well, never knowing truly how
far it goes down?
Who am I then?
What then becomes the thing holding me back if I don't
have you to blame?

Because while our fighting can be exhausting
And our sweetness sometimes fleeting
The laughter is long lasting
And the loving is comforting

It's difficult to watch you deadhead our flowers in the little
garden we planted together
Because it reminds me that to encourage growth, you
must cut back ruthlessly
flowers don't stay in bloom forever
And sometimes you need to cut off blossom you once
admired so deeply
so that they become something you only remember

In fondness and in aching
In heartbreak and peacemaking
In dust settling and then forgetting

ELECTRIC BLUE CAR ON MARLBOROUGH AND HORNSEY LANE

On my way home
I spotted a woman staring into her phone camera
Wearing a brown cowboy hat
Singing along to the radio, carefree

And as I crossed the street, two beautiful men drove past
and smiled at me
so I smiled back
And for the briefest moment felt assured that I could have
a passing connection with men
Other men
Even if shyly
Free from our bodies or desires
And from the expectations of how men should behave
when others are around to see

And as I continued across the street
feeling sound and walking lightly
I heard them laugh at the top of their lungs

Were they laughing at me?

LOVERS

You and I are the lovers drawn on the card
The same ones who fall from the Tower
Who find themselves impaled by seven swords or in The
Garden or in the
shower
of stars that fall on our heads
When you finally lead me to our bed

But do you know what is to become of me?
therefore, what is to become of you?
To shine so bright, you could not believe
that I could possibly burn right through you?
I'm a star
Can't you feel it?
I'm burning right through you and you can't even feel it?
Collateral damage for a life worth living
To be loved or admired, or a life worth remembering

II.

Oh, Father Ed wanted me dead
but all I wanted was to rest my head
underneath his robe, between his thighs
where only God was allowed

THOSE FACTORY WOMEN

Who was I five years ago?
Lavender laden in my oversized wool coat
So unattached from the inabilities of my throat
So far from the sea that I'd once wished to devote
Fully submerged in the water, never expecting to float

I feel no different from them now but I am smarter
I don't hold grudges and I don't miss the water
It swallowed me whole the last time I was deep within it
And scared me so much I swore I'd never go back in it
But instead now choose to lay next to it
And California's sun would bleach me blonde and I would
long for the streets I used to walk along
But this sun isn't an autumn sun, it's tricking us all
Just think back to last Tuesday when the snow began to
fall
and it didn't stop for a week
It then melted which then turned the snow into sleet
Everything was constantly changing
Even you and even me

Who you were when I fell in love with you back in 2007
Is a completely different person to the one who now
believes in heaven
I knew the ghost well because it had no home
and neither did I

I ran my fingers along the light pink linen
and felt close to the factory workers,
those factory women
In Lithuania
Content with making an item of quality, to be passed
down and cherished
I used to ask for more
dream of something more opulent, something more
garish

And I still have those same aspirations and those same
dreams
But when things began to unravel at the seams
It really makes you think
Have I gotten any closer to becoming the person I always
wanted to be?

PLATINUM SUMMER

I walked down to the Sherwin Williams where an old
crush worked
A beautiful man who remained distant, keeping me close
but never fully giving in
Never adoring me as much I him
So I decided he owed me one
Payment for my time and energy for a can of paint in the
shade of 'Romance'
Something he couldn't afford me in practice
but could steal from the local shop he worked at
So while standing on my mattress
I painted my walls a light salmon pink,
feminine enough directing me
towards the life I wanted to lead
No longer worried what people would think
Brush stroke by brush stroke; a sense of armour come over
me

Irving
Irving
Irving

My own little piece of heaven
Just off Judah, right in the middle of 11th
Down the road from the massive church of similar colour
That was the beginning of my platinum summer

I met you in the first week of June
our first trip to the sea mirrored by a sky so blue
On that unusually hot day at Baker Beach
I see it now clearer than ever
That day in my mind long in the sun lasting forever
Losing myself in the brief joy
So much so that I ignored the warning signs

My body sending me small messages through little jerks
and auras
Staying out all day and up all night
Much to my body's dismay and its own plight
The next morning, I knew something was wrong
my brain sending tiny shocks through my body
misfired electric currents or pulsating misconnections
happening neurologically
I've never been able to properly describe my epilepsy
Just sensations and vague descriptors in an attempt to
place it even adjacently

To save face, I decided to play it down
I calmly turned to you and said,
"I'm not feeling very well.
I'll first make you breakfast and then we'll go down to my
pharmacy to pick up my meds"
Not sure if I should even leave my bed
But I did and made my way to my little yellow kitchen that
I shared with four others
and began to cook you eggs
on the stovetop like my mother used to cook me when I
was younger
And as I looked upon the creamy contents of the shallow
frying pan
I locked eyes on the flame
Turned around and simply said your name

That's the last thing I remember from those few hours

I have since found that that moment of release
The moment where my body finally gives in to the current
that refuses to cease
The lightning strike hitting my head finally putting me at
ease
Is the only time I ever feel at true peace

True freedom, to me, is when you're able to exist with no
fear

Think about it this way:
I live my life every single day with the worry hanging over
my head
that at any moment my body will give in to itself
And find myself laying flat on the tan coloured bedspread
When the lights go dim and feedback fills my ears
A quick panic then soothing calm familiar through the years
Giving in to the violence my body is willing to put itself
through
I am no longer in control
Like reaching some sort of fucked up Shangri-La
With no conscious idea of the havoc that's taking its toll
On my body, my mind or my soul
A very short lived paradiso

Trying to recreate and recount a story I wasn't fully
conscious for is a difficult task to undertake
I can tell you in great detail the moments leading up to
and the rest I could try to fake
I've been told that when I came to, I stared at you
Terrified
Like a fawn, doe-eyed and drawn
But the next thing I actually remember was being walked
down the stairs of the Victorian I lived in
Arm-in-arm with a blonde medic
After that?
Being in some hallway in that hospital on Parnassus
My tongue bloody and raw from chewing or biting
Apparently you, I and the tiles of my kitchen were covered
in that same blood
we spread it around in a circle
But everything else? I couldn't tell you
I'm just not able

I feel far from that person who once had a crystal vision of the direction their life was going
Now moments of clarity are far more fleeting
Trudging through the fog of my mind or of the streets I walked through that summer to get here
May through September continues to be a time of trial and error
Running through the quiet and the terror
Sometimes relinquishing control and forgetting my tether
But whenever I feel metallic in the light coloured amber
I remind myself
While I may not always have you, or romance and I'm well past that platinum summer
that feeling is living within me, no need to try and remember
What's left is just the beating of those electric currents pulsating forever

III.

Moonflower, you bloomed!
Beautifully and slowly
Shame you'll be gone soon

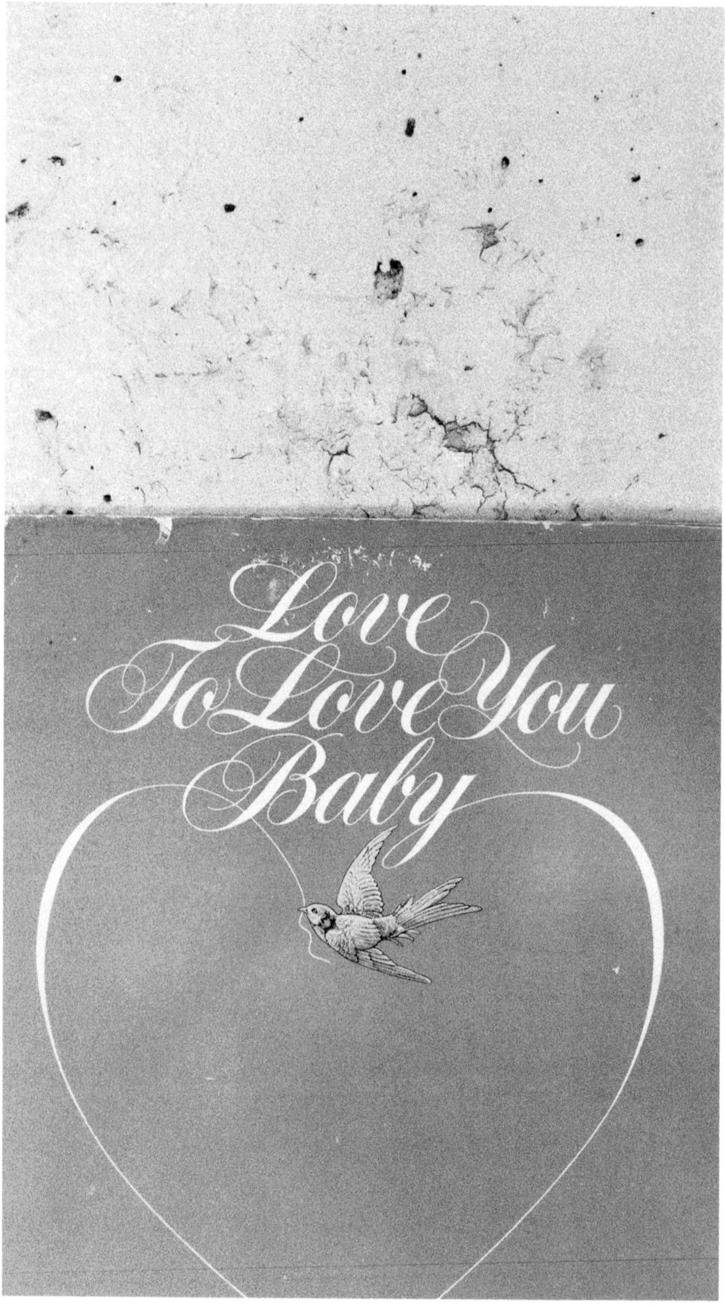
Love
To Love You
Baby

ON THE DAY WE TURNED 5

Drunk on three small glasses of red sparkling wine
I saw ourselves clearly for the first time
In the bright blue of the evening light
his pink body on our pink sheets
And his eyes were always bluest when he'd just finished
crying
For us and for himself
but mostly for himself
But probably because he caught me lying
Five years isn't much in the larger scheme of things
Not for wood or for glass or for flowers or for jewels
Or cheap pink candles that turned white
in the strong sunlight
which burned down to a pool
passing gulls crying in the sky
on the day that we turned 5

MALIBU

I think about Mike's Meat next to Casey's in the old
barbers
And your face in those reflective waters
Now when my shoes get soaked through the wet fallen
leaves
I put myself back in Malibu, my feet sinking through the
beach
And when I listen to music
I try not to let the songs colour my world with their
painted words
But it's hard
Sometimes it feels like I've never had a single original
thought

Now the street I walk towards smells of burnt sugar
bittersweet caramel
And it reminds me of those times I drove fast or rode a
bike without
putting the breaks on
finally brave
Embracing the wind and embracing the waves
And realizing I have no control
Because sometimes letting the world wash over you and
being open can
lead you to new experiences
or having your heart broken
But the excitement is in following the road less taken
In not knowing outcomes and in leaving the things you
should say,
spoken

CALIFORNIA

I woke up today at 7
That's early for me,
but not for most in my profession
See, most bakers rise early

But when I woke up today, the sky was sherbet orange
A sort of sweet red
And for a moment, I thought I was back home
Back in California

See, the Golden State is now shades of red
and all around it, wildlife dead
Last year it was the fires in the Palisades
that burned the rich people's mansions down in spades

But today I woke up in my little flat 5,000 miles away
and felt a pull to my home with the strongest of aches
We share the same sky
But mine's Shepherd's delight
And yours, the shade of the wildfires ravaging the
countryside

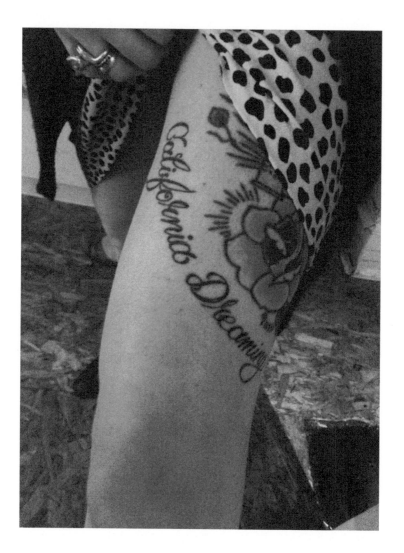

IV.

I think about my sadness a lot
I write around it, in these poems
I wonder if it will ever stop

THE LOVE OF A FOOL ON FIRE

The love of a fool on fire is the only love worth having or
life worth living
You'd be lucky enough to have it even for a while

My God fearing angel
I felt your trepidation when I finally took you in my mouth
Shaking with excitement as the further from heaven and
your preferred grandmother's arms you got
Feeling the strong pull of the south

You only felt free by the sea lined with cypress trees
White sandy beach
Carmel-by-the-sea
Moon beggar
But Mars shining down on you

But eventually I found that no love is perfect
And pure bliss is briefly lived
While hardships exist like fine web in the breeze
Only to be seen when the sun is cast upon them
Disturbed by the most unnerving of ease

Well hey,
That's no way to say goodbye
Tearing each other apart until the sound of the leaves and
tiny birds crying
are the only sounds left

Til then it's you
Bathed in orange
Making my porridge
The wrong way, of course, but lovingly no less
And me
peeling garlic cloves
for the lunch I will make us
Which will turn into leftovers
That we will never finish

MY THERAPIST TELLS ME I'M MAKING GREAT STRIDES

Everyone is a potential threat
To my lovers, sadly I am not your Pet
Or Sweetie or Darling
Or any other cute name
I cannot be fully yours until I've figured out your game
Learned the rules and figured out how to cheat
Apologies in advance but I can't afford to be beat
And even if you fall for some altered version of me
At least you'll have fallen for some part of me

And all of the things I've yet to unpack
Don't worry, I've shoved that stuff way in the back
And when those boxes begin to moan with pain
I might take a look at them again and learn self love isn't in
vain

Chains that rattle don't keep you up in the way you'd think
they would
They just tug and writhe, heavy on the chest
leave you exhausted, sometimes briefly happy
but forever restless

LIVE FLESH

Why do my legs scare you?
Why does the sight of my live flesh
Tan and free
Worry you but make your heart beat
faster, then quicker?
More than you're willing to admit
So your instant reaction is vitriol because you feel like you
might be committing a sin

But today I chose temptation instead of fear
And looked back at you grinning ear to ear
Catch you off guard and on the off chance that
we might briefly connect with each other free from this
world and the smell of fruit stands we pass like citrus
I'll see in your gaze simply for what it is
No hate, just pure desire
burning inside you much like the pyre
you set aflame for yourself and the man you wished you
could be

So instead I stoke the flame
because I refuse to take the blame
of a lifetime of your own personal shame
And catch the glint in your eye saying
"I'd wish you'd stay
and take me from this life of lying"
But I keep on walking and leave you hiding

Instead you chose to laugh at me
And I have no pity for a man who chose deflection
I see you for who you are and through all of your deception
So let this live bare flesh sear the corners of your mind
while you carry on the mundanities of your daily life

350 TRANS PEOPLE WERE MURDERED IN 2020

I say each of their names quietly to myself
Pronounce every syllable, no more pain to quell

I beat my chest for Tony
and turn my wrist for Monika
Clasp my hands for Merci
and lay my shirt for Nina

And for Marilyn who I never knew
but grew up in the same town as me
I cry for you
I write this for you

I say each of their names quietly to myself
Pronounce every syllable, no more pain to quell

V.

Everything feels like last year but nothing is the same
I'm listening to the same ten songs on repeat but have
since forgotten your name
I'm wearing the same brown coat I took from our closet
but wear different shoes for the rain
Everything feels like last year but everything has changed

ANGELS DON'T COME

Angels don't come
In the middle of the night or in the middle of a fight
They don't hold your arms behind you when you begin to
act reckless
Or stop the crows feathers from blowing in the cold wind,
breathless
Angels don't come
when you're about to say something you're sure to regret
They just stare, gold gilded
Waiting for you to take the next wrong step
Angels don't come because they are not our guardians or
our makers
They're just a figment of who we wish would help us when
we make mistakes we wish to be forgotten later
Angels, adorned in taffeta and shrouded in a head of soft
brown curls
Masking their look of contentment as they watch us cry
like a little girl
the devil was an angel too, and he was once beautiful and
had good intentions
before realizing it was a lot more fun to watch us be
tempted by vices
than to steer us in the right direction

CANYON

The Palisades in flames in view
Smoke billowing,
seen from the coast of Malibu
That pit in my stomach, I threw to the wind
The sea air felt cool driving down the coast,
wind battering my skin
The sunlight on my face healing
California, my kin

Then driving through Laurel Canyon late at night
Music so loud, remembering lyrics and not driving off the
cliff our only plights
With my girl by my side and her impaired sight
Sees me for who I am
And from her I can't hide
Holding a mirror to me
Who I see, I can't help but like

Because
I'm raging, I'm electric, I'm Daddy, I'm strong
I'm quiet, I'm fading, I'm baby, I'm small

DINNER

A millionaire bought my dinner the other day
I acted like the stupid bitch they believe me to be
I made them laugh
Batted my eyes

"Provocateur" they call me

I chose the steak
It was worth it

HEAVEN OR LAST VEGAS

The smell of smoke always reminds me of the birthdays
I had at the park across the road from my house
And how I imagined laying in the tall grass felt like being
in the Sahara
my own dry desert
Near the trailer park with fake green grass that I think
was across from a pervert
All of these images I see
Developed like film, in Kodak, in sets of three
Remembered like summers passed
Quick snapshots that were made to last
But memory is often fraught
Lost and fleeting in our thoughts
And we remember them a little differently each time
So what is the truth and what is the rhyme
and reason to what has happened, what we think has
happened and what we wanted to happen

'Heaven or Last Vegas'
It was a misprint on the program at your service
Oscar you're there now and who knows how
you arrived
But you did, and hopefully at peace
finally
Lilith beside you
In memory

KILL YOUR DARLINGS

I love the saying 'Kill your darlings'
because it insinuates a brutal cutting off of something
that means so much to you
In writing, sure
But in life? Vital
For me, those are the ways in which I allow myself to be
hurt over and over again

So I'll kill every single one of those darlings off
one by one
Until every last bad habit I tended to so carefully
has been thrown to the trough
And fed to pigs who haven't eaten in days
Till the men I once loved but never loved me back can't be
seen through the haze
And the only clear vision in my rear view
Will be the mess that I made, then trudged through
to get here

So kill your darlings
It's freeing and fun
Kill every single last one of them until there's only one
You
a vision in blue
The aftermath of bloodshed projected in Bellevue
Till your life is the way you've always wanted to live it, no way
for others to misconstrue
Rid yourself of the shame that's always followed you
from the time you were a child and destroyed everything
you knew
And came to love with an innocence only a child can bring to

So kill those darlings, one by one
It sounds hard but it's actually pretty fun
First, find your target
then cock your gun

Go on, what have you got to lose?
Knock each of them off until there's only one

AM I A ROSE?

Am I a rose?
Am I the flower that gets to have not one season but two?
The flower that everyone awaits until they finally bloom?
The flower that starts out bare as a bush that looks like it
doesn't have much to give
Only to impress and be the muse for as many poems as
there are artists that have ever lived?

Am I a rose?
Whose beauty is admired and not just considered but
respected?
That people stop their busy days to appreciate and think
of often?
That once my petals fall and am left with nothing but the
stem
Surprise the passerby with a brick red fruit at its hem

Whose rosehips eventually meet your lips
through syrup and maybe jam
Am I a flower good enough to cut from your garden and
put on your nightstand?

If roses are flowers that have the look of flowers that are
looked at,
Then I would want to the one, the one you think of often
Because roses don't compare themselves to any other, not
peonies or cosmos on windowsills
They live and breathe and bloom and exist as they should
Of their own free will
While wildflowers persist in their own unique way
they scald and fry in the sun's rays
their petals too delicate to persevere in the same way

While roses thrive in the light and withstand the heat
and the frost
Beat the harsh summers and winters, their beauty never
exhausts

But to question if you are the rose
You already believe it not to be true
And I don't need to ask who
And I don't need to ask you
You will love me for the bloom
And even so the prick
You will give me to others
For when they are sad or when they are sick
Because I am the rose
I answer my own curiosity with my own prose
I'll bloom and whither to fruit
Come hither
And endure and persevere winter after winter

CRY BABY CRY

The only way through it
is through it
of course millions of teenage girls could tell you that much
That after a heartbreak they once felt they'd never survive
Can look back now and genuinely feel alive
Free of the ache that black snake moaned them to the
chains of a first love
reminisce and laugh that once push came to shove
They survived
those girls were so much braver than I
they cried out loud instead of trying to hide

But I must remind myself they also had a head start
Held tenderly by a world that embraced their love for the
school boy that broke their heart
So while their heads were gently cradled through a thin
veil of mesh and pearls
I was left to fend on my own, raging thrashing and other
forms of coping to exist in this cruel world

So now here I am at 28
Attempting to undo the mess that childhood made
Unpicking nails that were left in the crates
but I'll get there in the end, no matter how late
And love myself and kiss myself and be happier
more than I could have ever dreamed
Because confronting demons of the past isn't as hard as it
may have once seemed

I'll survive too
Through this mess, once your angel, even with a heart
broken in two
Learn from those girls, weeping in their bedrooms
Experiencing grief so real you couldn't convince them that
they'd ever make it through

So cry baby, cry
hold onto each other through this tough life
wipe each other's tears and learn from each other's fears
and keep on loving until the day we die

VI.

my head hung out of the taxi
like a dog
Blissfully
The warm air hit my face and blew through my hair
And for a second I forgot what year it was
and I was just happy

We drove by a billboard that was the length of an entire
building that read:
YOU CAN HAVE ANYTHING IF YOU CAN DREAM IT

I laughed and felt amused
because stupidly or not, I believe it to be true

THE SAME WATER YOU WADE IN

Summer boy swimming in the summer rain
oh my god, I can actually see your pain
it trails behind you like slick oil only shown by the sunlight
like the shame you carry always close by
in the river glittering softly, shimmering high

You crawled into my bed
not in a blue swimsuit
but in crisp, white underwear and nothing else
Because you thought I could take your sadness away
And stupidly I thought I could
But you keep your sadness close
It's the closest anyone will ever get to you

and even though I feel your sticky skin lonely at night
there'd always be a barrier between you and I
you say you set up mirrors in your garden so you can see
yourself posing
but I know it's because you need all angles present just
incase the shame is lurking
with no mother or lover
I can be both but your sadness has replaced your mother
and cradles you tenderly in the night
it's easier than standing directly in the light
deflect while it reflects upon that same water you wade in
it's the same water you wait in
Moss beneath your feet you felt comfortable to put your
weight in
but slip and lose your balance while you're patiently
waiting

they say drowning is a peaceful way to die
losing consciousness and giving into the tide
if you see God, will you tell him hi
from me?

VII.

Is that a sore throat?
Or was it the way you fucked my face so hard I was left in a
daze
And after you left, I cried because I felt used
because I fell for your charm and your eyes that looked blue
in the lights where we met but I never caught your name
And even when I wanted it over, I still wanted you to stay
And wished how after I'd finish wiping you off of my face,
you'd stop to ask me about my day

But anyways
I have your number
We should do this again
Maybe then I could convince you to be my friend
And the next time we meet up you might kiss me on my
mouth
and tell me I look beautiful before pushing my head south

BLUE MADONNA

Can I just be beautiful
and be the doll which everyone expects me to be?
Take the clocks off the wall and the dried sage off the
twine so I can use the leaves
You don't even need to be kind
Just want to live the life that is only mine
Not for you
to inspect or to approve

My man, it's violence
and it's all around me
My John, the dissonance
because your desire betrays me
I cannot be your Madonna
your mother, your maker
I can only be the fantasy
you don't want me as your homemaker

I cannot stand on the street
I'm a moving target and stopping would leave me
vulnerable
because you will not leave me in peace
Until you see every last one of my kin's bleeding meat
and bones in suitcases and black bin bags
But you cannot take my life, I'm not yet the earth's to have

Because it's not enough for me to be beautiful
Beautiful enough as to not catch your attention
It is simply the fact that I exist
and your mistaken belief that I would not be missed

Blue Madonna
Oh my angel
who inhabits not one spirit but two
you never wanted this burden
you just wanted to be free

VIII.

I forgive you for calling me a cunt
And I forgive you for making it worse when you tried to
make me feel better
I forgive you for that time you took me to that plastic log
cabin
And I forgive you for allowing that to happen
I forgive you for forgetting to call and leaving my
messages unanswered
And I forgive you for never acknowledging the time I came
out to you in that handwritten letter
I forgive you for embarrassing me in front of our friends
And I forgive you for your loving having a limit

SYLVIA

Summer
Platinum Summer
a time in San Francisco usually shrouded in fog, finally
she saw the clearest path
Like a dark night lit up by a lightening strike
an apparition, like a vision
Sylvia Plath

After her first suicide attempt decidedly tried on
happiness for size
and dyed her hair platinum blonde
Before she escaped to the beyond
Before it was only her memory and words that lived on
and on
She tried a home dye job for Ted
Before she laid the kids to bed
with towels stuffed under the door
before her porcelain white thighs rested on the kitchen
floor

just a single photograph of her fair-skinned face smiling
on the beach
just two lovers and a beachcomber by the real sea

But there's no dissolving a sadness like hers, only managing
She learned that in the end
and pointed her black patent shoes away from the ocean
and in that same fragility which also felt like drowning
found strength, she needed no men
Just the black waters flooding in from the ocean
Hugging her body tightly with nothing but devotion
But until then

Happy, smiling, blonde and beautiful
and I will try to do the same, be the dutiful
Mother, lover, carer, friend
I'll do it for Sylvia, until I meet my own end
but I hope to learn from her what she could not do for herself
and find the beauty in imperfection, in one's sadness
and the power in one's self

YOUR WIFE AND I ARE NOT THE SAME

Your family had sweet paper decorations hanging in your
newly fruiting cherry trees
that blew gently in the soft summer breeze
All I had was you standing before me
while I was on my knees

CALIFORNIA SWEET

Blood
I taste blood whenever I think of you
Blood like holy wine slowly running through
like citrus through my veins
like those lazy summer days
that moved quickly in a daze
in those big shirts and shorts I used to hate
til I saw them on you

California sweet
in your California sweat
after our California death
Love, Your California Mess
candy hard you were
impossible to bite
but soft and dripping when you finally threw your ribbons
through those California skies

perfect
It could have never have been me
Could've been those peonies
but not me when I was nineteen

My hand
I place my hand upon them those hydrangea that grow
late summer to fall
and I feel soft and supple like I once did in your arms
but no more
California sweet we were
for two weeks, at most four
But I guess that saccharine behind the cheek punch
doesn't last long after all

BLUE FOREVER

I walked by these yellow dahlias in someone's front garden
illuminated only by the evening's all consuming cerulean
sky and it reminded me of you and I
Forever glowing even without sunshine
you, blue forever
me, bright through whatever weather

ACKNOWLEDGEMENTS

Firstly, I want to say thank you to Peter Collins at Polari Press for collaborating on this project with me. I had a painfully specific vision for this book and Peter was along for the ride but always up for the challenge and incredibly generous with their time and energy and passion.

A deep and profound thanks to Tahnee Cadrez Freda, for being my eyes, ears and heart. As the person who has painstakingly read and helped edit each of these poems and their many iterations, I feel most grateful to her. She never stopped believing in me and the work.

Thank you to Paul Kindersely, for being a generous spirit and brilliant artist. A constant inspiration in resilience and staying true to oneself, in art and real life.

My beautiful parents, Frances and Jose Luis Ramirez for their unwavering support in so many forms. I'm constantly astounded by their love and generosity.

Thank you to Hal Haines, Harry Clayton-Wright, Amelia Abraham, Edmund Shaw, Jamie Luke Scoular, KT Nelson, Alex Mein, Alan Wyffels, David Michon, John Booth, Deidre Corda, Chelsea Pipkin, Iva Aijder and Wilfrid Wood, Jess Blackstone, Mat Appleton for your support, encouragement, friendship and collaboration.

Last but not least, thank you to my husband, Daniel Thurman. If I began to list all I was grateful for it would be ridiculous, but mostly thank you for the laughs, the inspiration and the love.

POLARI PRESS

Taking our name from the secret slang Polari, we are an independent publishing house which seeks out hidden voices and helps them be heard.

Although Polari was spoken almost exclusively by gay and bisexual men, the nature of clandestine meetings of the mid 1900s, when homosexuality was still criminalised, brought together people from all walks of life who all had an influence on the language.

Cockney, Romany and Italian languages mixed with the colloquialisms of thespians, circus performers, wrestlers, sailors and wider criminal communities to create a slang to express their sexuality secretly and safely.

Inspired by these origins, we publish queer voices as well as other marginalised groups, to share our perspectives with each other, and help build a collaborative platform for all of us.

polari.com

Adriann Ramirez grew up in El Centro, California close to the Mexican border before ultimately moving to London in 2016. They began making short films in San Francisco while working towards their degree in dance and choreography, while simultaneously working as a principal dancer with PUSH Dance Company in 2013. Their first short film, *California Dreamin'*, premiered at the 2014 Frameline International LGBTQ Film Festival and went on to show at various film festivals around the USA and UK. In 2018, they created a podcast called *Lavender Language*, an ongoing series of conversations where they speak with queer artists about their creative process and how they maintain careers in artistic fields. *Hot Tears Through Velvet Rage* is their first book.

adriannramirez.com

PHOTO BY JAMIE LUKE SCOULAR